Totally WACKY FACTS ABOUT the HUMAN BODY

CARI MEISTER

CAPSTONE PRESS
a capstone imprint

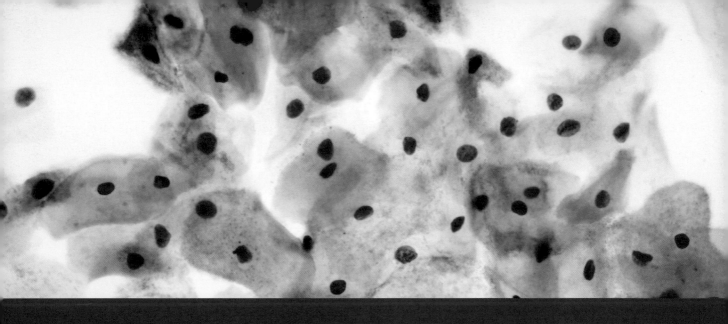

The body has **200** types of cells, including those found in our blood, skin, and muscles.

50-100 TRILLION:
the number of cells in an adult's body

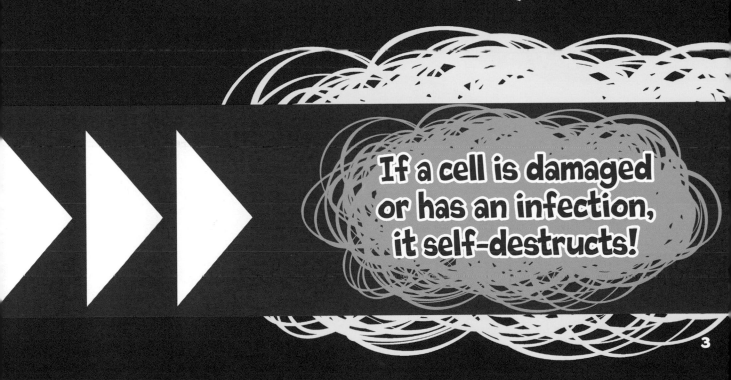

If a cell is damaged or has an infection, it self-destructs!

MUSCLE CELLS LIVE AS LONG AS YOU DO.

Skin cells live for one to 30 days.

WHITE BLOOD CELLS LIVE FOR LESS THAN ONE DAY!

Skin is your body's LARGEST ORGAN.

WITHOUT SKIN YOU WOULD EVAPORATE.

40 POUNDS

(18 KILOGRAMS): THE AMOUNT OF SKIN YOU WILL SHED IN YOUR LIFETIME

MUSCLES IN THE HUMAN BODY: 639

You use 200 muscles to take one step!

MUSCLES MAKE UP HALF OF YOUR WEIGHT.

8

To kiss, a person uses 34 FACIAL MUSCLES.

You have 206 bones in your body—106 of them are in your hands and feet.

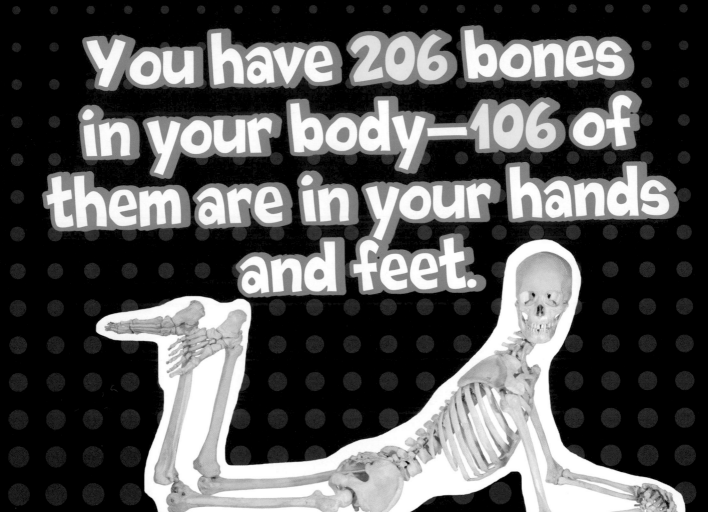

YOUR FEMUR (THIGHBONE) IS THE STRONGEST BONE IN YOUR BODY.

Bones are stronger than concrete!

THE AVERAGE NUMBER OF BROKEN
BONES A PERSON HAS IN A
LIFETIME IS TWO.

Want to keep your
bones strong?
Drink more MILK!

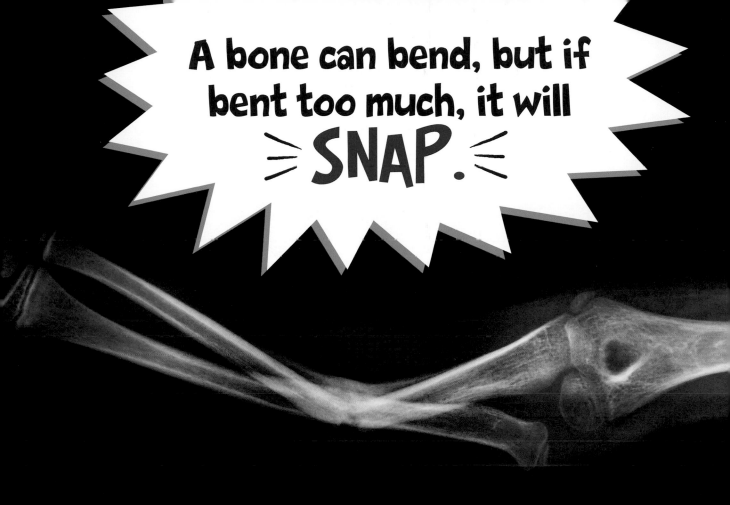

A bone can bend, but if bent too much, it will ≥SNAP.≤

Your teeth are the only bones that can't repair themselves.

Your baby teeth grew before you were born—they were just hiding beneath your gums.

ABOUT ONE BABY IN 2,500 IS BORN WITH A TOOTH SHOWING.

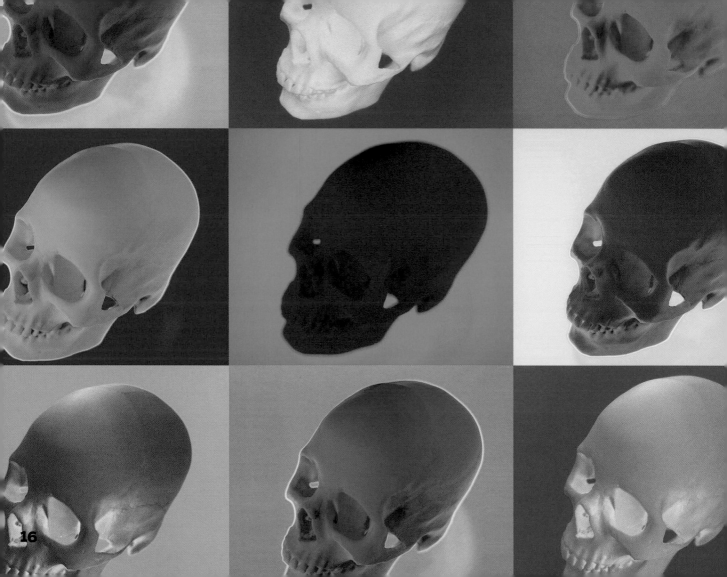

AN ADULT'S SKULL IS MADE UP OF 22 BONES.

Your brain is active while YOU SLEEP.

About **80%** of your brain is **WATER.**

THE BRAIN CANNOT FEEL PAIN.

19

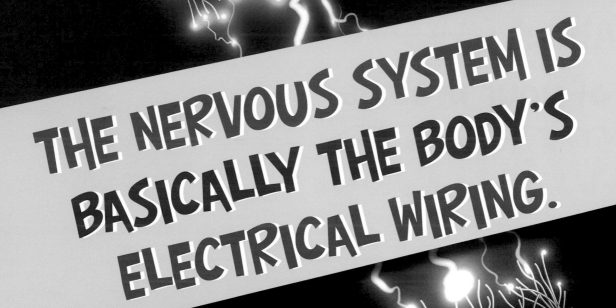

THE NERVOUS SYSTEM IS BASICALLY THE BODY'S ELECTRICAL WIRING.

Neurons send signals through the nervous system that travel at about 328 feet (100 meters) per second!

Your brain has about 100 billion neurons in it!

A human **EYE** has a **LENS** that works very much like a **CAMERA LENS.**

Your **EYES** are made mostly of a jelly-like goop.

YOU BLINK ABOUT 6,205,000 TIMES IN ONE YEAR!

23

SOME PEOPLE CAN HEAR THEIR EYEBALLS MOVING.

24

EXOPHTHALMOS
IS A CONDITION IN WHICH A PERSON'S EYEBALLS BULGE.

SOME PEOPLE ARE BORN WITHOUT IRISES—THE COLORED PARTS OF THE EYES.

ALMOST ALL ADULTS HAVE **MITES** LIVING ON THEIR EYELASHES.

MITES

Some people have two rows of EYELASHES.

YOUR THUMB IS THE SAME SIZE AS THE LENGTH OF YOUR NOSE.

Your ears and nose never stop growing.

YOUR NOSE IS MADE OF CARTILAGE—THE SAME STUFF THAT MAKES UP A SHARK'S SKELETON.

Some people snore louder than the sound of a **JACKHAMMER** on cement!

60% OF MEN OVER AGE 60 SNORE.

ZZZZ

33

Despite a widely-held belief, your hair cannot turn white from shock.

Hair grows faster in warmer weather.

34

Less than 2 percent of people in the world have red hair.

YOUR HAIR IS DEAD. THAT'S WHY IT DOESN'T HURT WHEN YOU CUT IT.

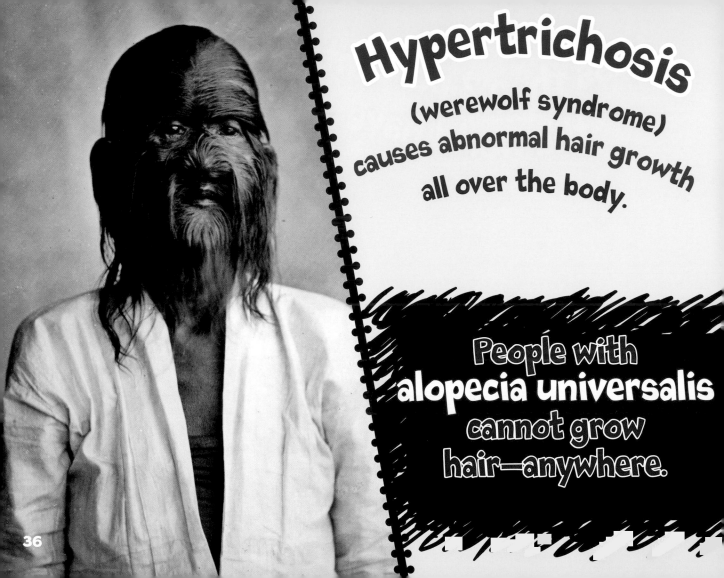

Hypertrichosis

(werewolf syndrome) causes abnormal hair growth all over the body.

People with **alopecia universalis** cannot grow hair—anywhere.

BLONDES HAVE MORE HAIR THAN PEOPLE WITH OTHER HAIR COLORS.

EVERY DAY YOU LOSE ABOUT 75 STRANDS OF HAIR.

LIPS DO NOT SWEAT.

YOUR LIPS GET THINNER AS YOU GET OLDER.

Very thin skin covers lips. The blood underneath the skin makes lips look red!

YOUR TONGUE IS ONE OF THE STRONGEST MUSCLES IN YOUR BODY.

The longest tongue ever recorded was 3.97 inches (10 centimeters).

EVERY TONGUE PRINT IS UNIQUE.

No one is exactly sure why we yawn.

People yawn more during winter.

SOME SCIENTISTS BELIEVE WE YAWN TO COOL DOWN THE BRAIN.

Most yawns last about 6 seconds.

YOU HAVE ABOUT **9,000** TASTE BUDS ON YOUR **TONGUE.**

There are also taste buds on the inside of your cheeks.

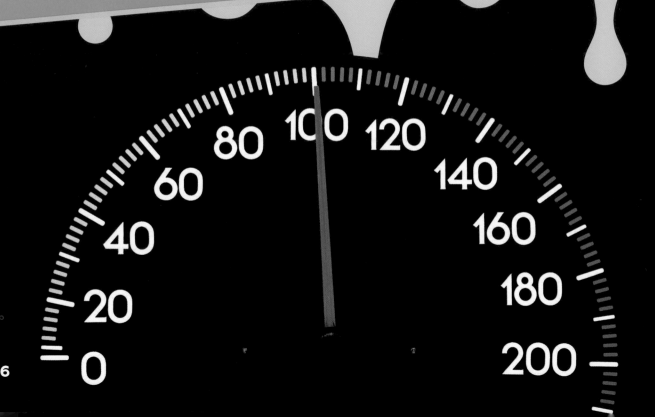

A sneeze can travel up to 100 miles per hour (161 kilometers per hour).

46

Donna Griffiths, a **12-YEAR-OLD** from England, sneezed for **978** days in a row!

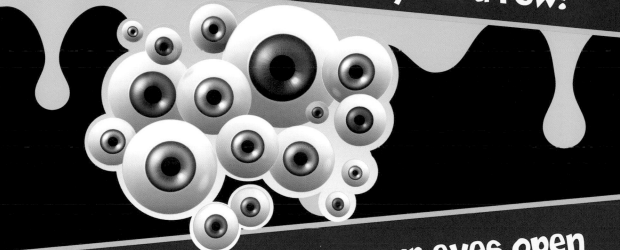

It is impossible to keep your eyes open when you sneeze.

IF A MAN NEVER CUT HIS BEARD, IT COULD GROW TO BE 30 FEET (9.1 M) LONG IN HIS LIFETIME.

WHEN YOU'RE SCARED, YOUR EARS MAKE EXTRA EARWAX.

Earwax is not really wax. It's a mix of oil, sweat, hair, and dead skin.

SOME PEOPLE BELIEVE THAT IF YOU HAVE STICKY EARWAX, YOU STINK!

AN AVERAGE HUMAN HEART WILL BEAT ABOUT **2.5 BILLION** TIMES IN A **LIFETIME.**

A heart can beat outside of a body for a short time.

YOUR HEART ISN'T REALLY RED. IT'S A **RED-BROWN** COLOR WITH PATCHES OF **YELLOW FAT**.

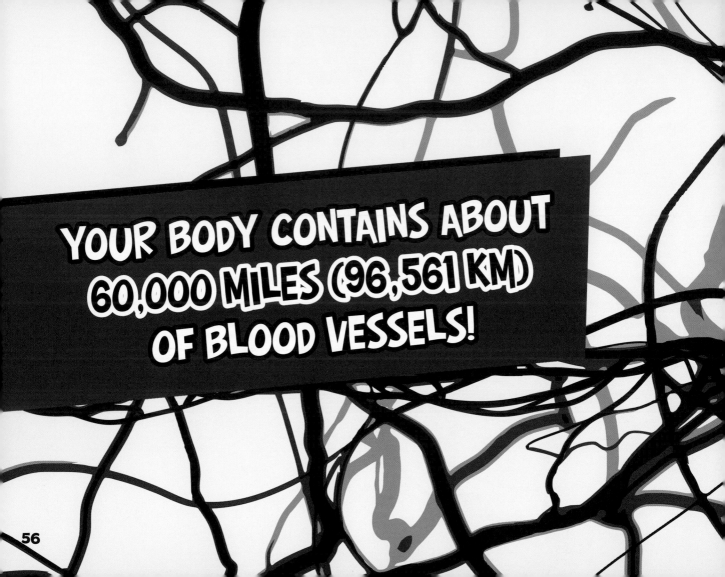

YOUR BODY CONTAINS ABOUT 60,000 MILES (96,561 KM) OF BLOOD VESSELS!

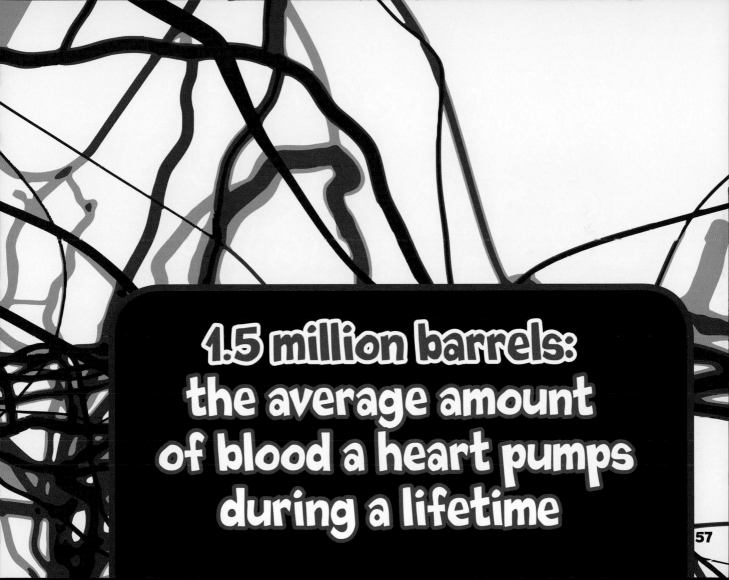

1.5 million barrels: the average amount of blood a heart pumps during a lifetime

You have about **25 TRILLION** red blood cells.

ONE DROP OF BLOOD HAS ABOUT **250 MILLION** RED BLOOD CELLS IN IT.

SOME PEOPLE CAN PLAY THE PIANO WITH THEIR TOES.

More than half of the world's population has one foot that is bigger than the other.

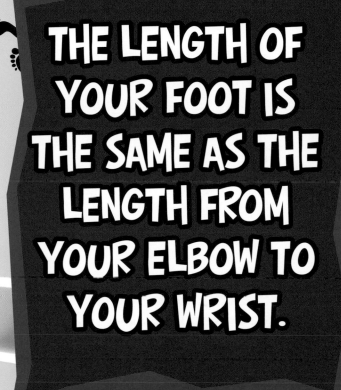

THE LENGTH OF YOUR FOOT IS THE SAME AS THE LENGTH FROM YOUR ELBOW TO YOUR WRIST.

Pig and cow heart valves can be used to replace bad heart valves in humans.

If you lose a finger, a toe can be sewn on to replace it.

Fingernails grow about **3 TO 4 TIMES** faster than toenails.

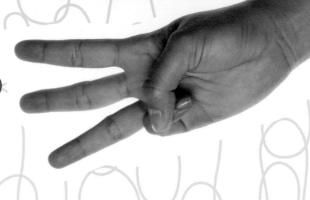

IF YOU LOSE A TOENAIL, IT MAY TAKE ONE YEAR FOR IT TO GROW BACK.

Nails curl when you let them grow very long.

MILLIONS OF TEENY, TINY CREATURES LIVE BENEATH YOUR NAILS.

65

You are tallest in the morning, because gravity pulls downward on your body throughout the day.

THE TALLEST MAN EVER WAS ROBERT WADLOW. HE MEASURED 8 FEET, 11 INCHES (2.7 METERS) TALL.

ASTRONAUTS

ARE 2 INCHES (5.08 CM) TALLER WHILE THEY ARE IN

SPACE.

LUNGS ARE SPONGY.

The left lung is smaller than the right lung.

The average person takes about 7 million breaths in one year.

YOU HAVE
1,000 MILES (1,609 KM)
OF AIRWAYS
IN YOUR BODY.

Sweat is like air-conditioning for your body.

Sweat doesn't smell. It's the bacteria that live near the sweat glands that **stink.**

MOST PEOPLE SWEAT ABOUT 278 GALLONS (1,052 LITERS) PER YEAR.

THERE ARE 500,000 SWEAT GLANDS IN YOUR FEET.

STRESSED OUT?

Your body makes a hormone called adrenaline when you're under stress.

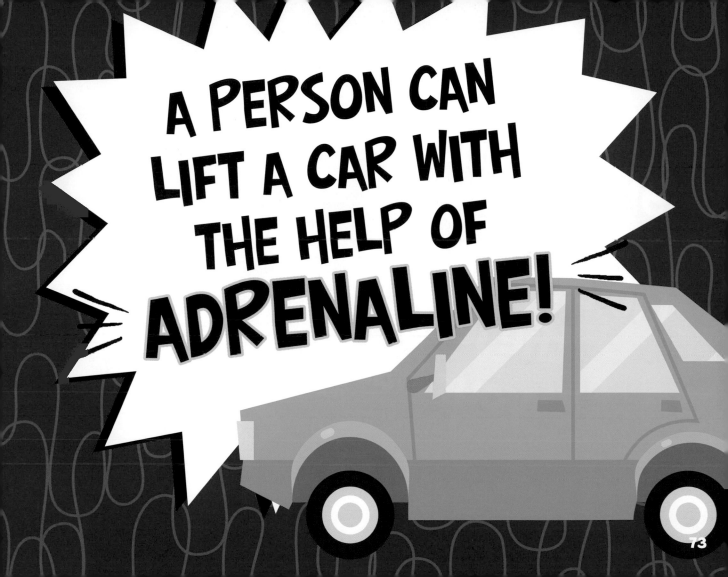

Your kidneys look like giant kidney beans. They're about 4 inches (10 cm) long, or about the length of your hand.

KIDNEYS FILTER ABOUT 50 GALLONS (189 L) OF BLOOD PER DAY. THAT'S ENOUGH TO FILL A LARGE TRASH CAN!

YOUR SPLEEN IS SOFT AND PURPLE AND IS ABOUT THE SIZE OF YOUR FIST.

YOU CAN LIVE WITHOUT YOUR SPLEEN.

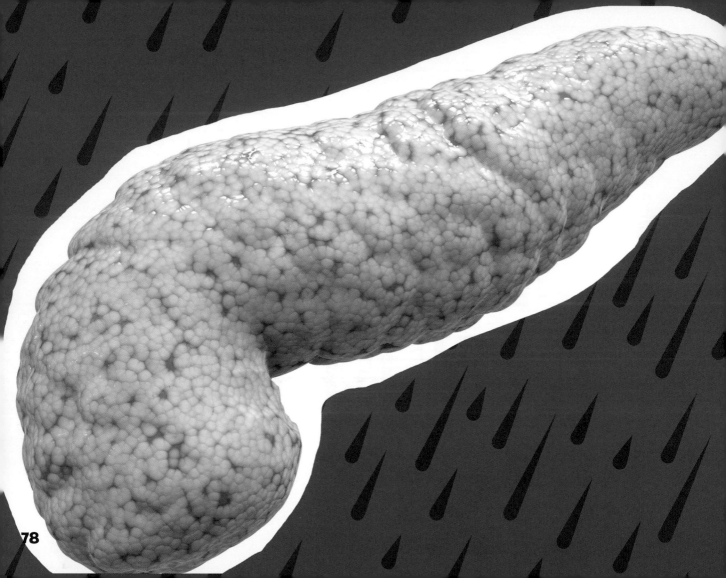

A PANCREAS IS SHAPED KIND OF LIKE A SKINNY SOCK.

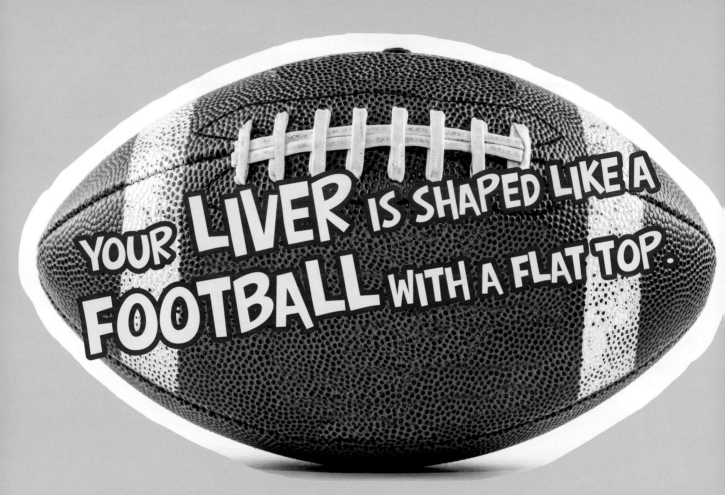

YOUR **LIVER** IS SHAPED LIKE A **FOOTBALL** WITH A FLAT TOP.

At 3½ POUNDS

(1.6 kg), the liver wins the title for the heaviest internal organ.

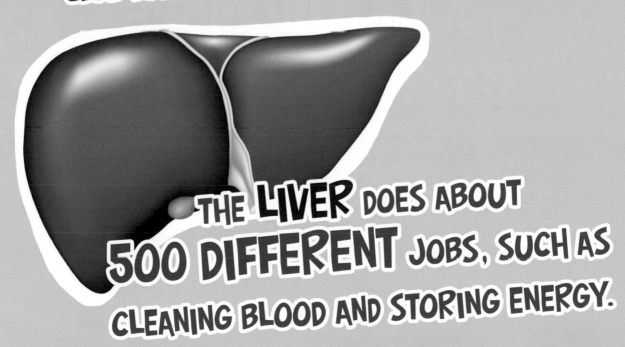

THE **LIVER** DOES ABOUT **500 DIFFERENT** JOBS, SUCH AS CLEANING BLOOD AND STORING ENERGY.

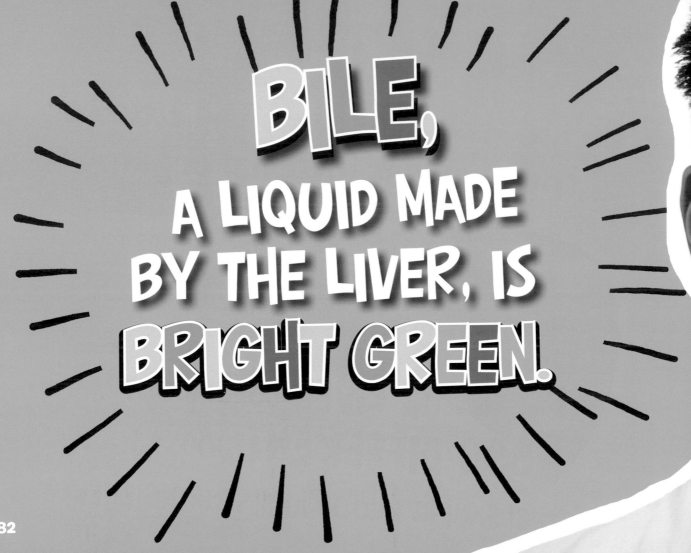

83

YOUR **BELLYBUTTON** IS REALLY A SCAR WHERE YOUR

UMBILICAL CORD WAS CUT.

THINK YOU'RE CLEAN?

MANY DIFFERENT KINDS OF BACTERIA LIVE INSIDE YOUR BELLYBUTTON!

YOU CAN LIVE ABOUT ONE WEEK WITHOUT WATER.

A PERSON CAN LIVE UP TO TWO MONTHS WITHOUT FOOD.

THE FOOD YOU EAT SPENDS ABOUT 2 TO 4 HOURS IN YOUR STOMACH.

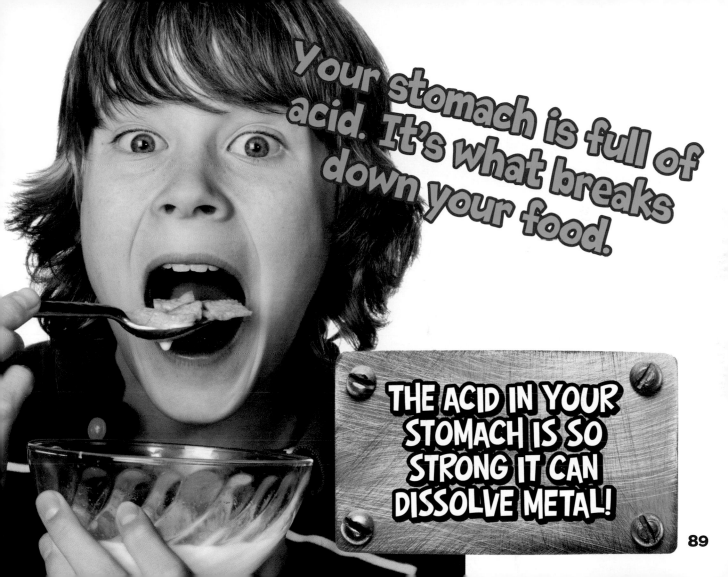

Your stomach is full of acid. It's what breaks down your food.

THE ACID IN YOUR STOMACH IS SO STRONG IT CAN DISSOLVE METAL!

89

IF COMPLETELY UNCOILED, YOUR INTESTINES WOULD BE ABOUT 25 FEET (7.62 M) LONG.

THAT'S ABOUT AS LONG

AS AN ORCA WHALE.

DID YOU KNOW THAT POOP CAN BE PURPLE OR BLUE?

You will poop about **7 TONS** (6.4 metric tons) in your lifetime.

The bladder is a bag made out of

STRETCHY MUSCLE.

WHEN YOUR BLADDER IS FULL, IT IS THE SIZE OF A GRAPEFRUIT.

95

You may have **6 BILLION** bacteria living in your mouth.

Some **BACTERIA** help you to digest foods. Other bacteria help protect your gums.

3 TO 5 POUNDS (1.36 TO 2.27 KG) THE AMOUNT OF BACTERIA THE AVERAGE PERSON CARRIES

EVERYBODY FARTS! SOME PEOPLE JUST DON'T ADMIT IT.

SODA AND GUM CAN MAKE YOU FART MORE.

Some people eat their **HAIR.**

THE LARGEST HAIR BALL REMOVED FROM A PERSON'S STOMACH WEIGHED 10 POUNDS (4.54 KG)!

YOU PROBABLY HAVE ENOUGH FAT IN YOUR BODY TO MAKE ABOUT 75 CANDLES.

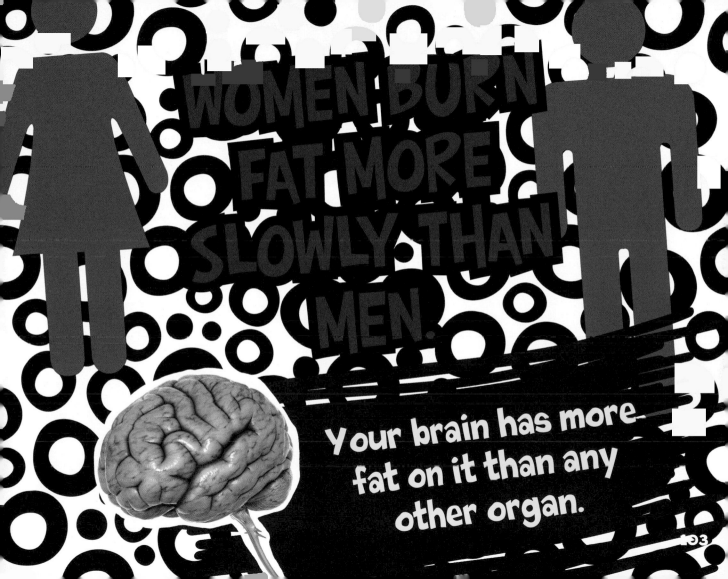

YOUR BODY MAKES ABOUT **3 SODA CANS** WORTH OF **PHLEGM** AND **MUCUS** PER DAY.

BURP!

THAT'S THE SOUND OF GAS MAKING YOUR ESOPHAGUS VIBRATE.

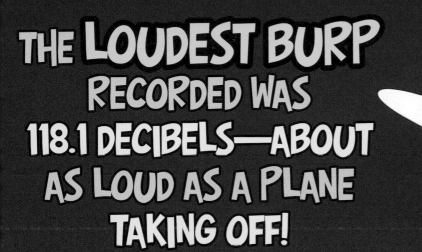

THE **LOUDEST BURP** RECORDED WAS 118.1 DECIBELS—ABOUT AS LOUD AS A PLANE TAKING OFF!

The faster you eat, the more gas you will have.

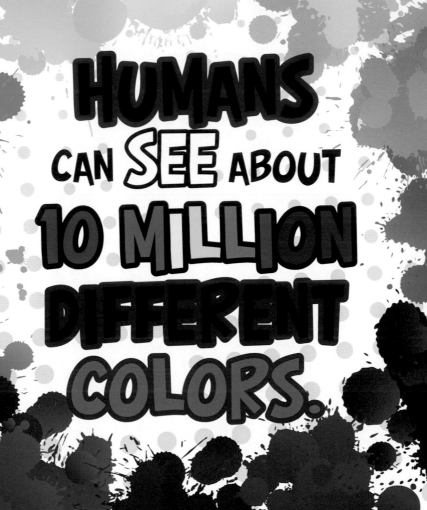

HUMANS CAN SEE ABOUT 10 MILLION DIFFERENT COLORS.

WE **HEAR** THINGS WHILE WE SLEEP, BUT OUR BRAINS DON'T DETECT THE SOUNDS.

THE NOSE CAN DETECT ABOUT 1 TRILLION DIFFERENT SMELLS.

GLOSSARY

bacteria—very small living things that exist all around you and inside you; some bacteria cause disease

bile—a green liquid made by the liver that helps digest food

cell—a basic part of an animal or plant that is so small you can't see it without a microscope

detect—to notice something; your sense organs detect things about your surroundings

esophagus—the tube that carries food from the mouth to the stomach; muscles in the esophagus push food into the stomach

filter—to remove unwanted materials

gland—an organ in the body that makes natural chemicals or helps substances leave the body

heart valve—part of the heart that opens and closes to let blood go in and come out

hormone—a chemical made by a gland in the body that affects a person's growth and development

liver—the organ responsible for making bile and storing body oils; the liver cleans blood and aids in digestion

neuron—a nerve cell

organ—a part of the body that does a certain job; your heart, lungs, and kidneys are organs

pancreas—an organ near the stomach that makes insulin

spleen—an organ that is part of the immune system and helps to remove blood cells

umbilical cord—the tube that connects an unborn baby to its mother

READ MORE

Barnhill, Kelly Regan. *The Wee Book of Pee.* The Amazingly Gross Human Body. Mankato, Minn.: Capstone Press, 2010.

Bradley, Timothy J. *Gross Anatomy.* Strange but True. Huntington Beach, Calif.: Teacher Created Materials, 2013.

Bredeson, Carmen. *Weird But True Human Body Facts.* Weird But True Science. Berkeley, N.J.: Enslow Elementary, 2011.

INTERNET SITES

FactHound offers a safe, fun way to find Internet sites related to this book. All of the sites on FactHound have been researched by our staff.

Here's all you do:

Visit *www.facthound.com*

Type in this code: 9781491483596

INDEX

Mind Benders are published by Capstone,
1710 Roe Crest Drive, North Mankato, Minnesota 56003
www.mycapstone.com

Editor: Shelly Lyons
Designer: Lori Bye
Media Researcher: Jo Miller

Library of Congress Cataloging-in-Publication Data
Cataloging-in-publication data is on file with the Library of Congress.
Meister, Cari, author.
Totally wacky facts about the human body / by Cari Meister.
Mind benders (Capstone Press)
North Mankato, Minnesota : Capstone, [2016] | Series: Mind benders
Audience: Ages 8-12.
Audience: Grades 4 to 6.
LCCN 2015031026
ISBN 978-1-4914-8359-6 (library binding : alk.paper)
ISBN 978-1-4914-8368-8 (paperback: alk. paper)
ISBN 978-1-4914-8370-1 (eBook pdf)
Human physiology—Miscellanea—Juvenile literature. | Human anatomy—Miscellanea—Juvenile literature.
LCC QM27 .M45 2016
DDC 612—dc23
LC record available at http://lccn.loc.gov/2015031026

Photo Credits

Alamy: The Natural History Museum, 36; Getty Images: Digital Vision, 16; Newscom: Everett Collection, 66, (right), REX/Philip Reeves, 65, Science Photo Library/Steve Gschmeissner, 26-27; Shutterstock: Air Images, 45, Aleks Melnik, 79, Aleksandr Bryliaev, 18, Alesikka, 42-43, Alexander Pekour, 95, AlexanderZe, 24, Andrey Armyagov, 25, art_of_sun, 20, ArtHeart, 62, Artishok, 63, Ben Schonewille, 74, bikeriderlondon, 96, Blamb, 94, blambca, 83, (right), block23, 19, C_Eng-WOng Photography, 80, Carlos Caetano, 43, chikapylka, 107, Constantine Pankin, 48, Coprid, 104, CREATISTA, 100, Darren Brode, 15, dedek, 91, Designua, 4, Dmitry Kalinovsky, 32, East, 8, Ebic, 67, Eldad Carin, 101, EMcgiq, 103, Gencho Petkov, 84, Gun2becontinued, 55, Haver, 60, HitToon.Com, 86, (right), i3alda, 86, (left), imageerinx, 47, Irina Mir, 92, James Bowyer, 46, Jezper, 97, Jiri Miklo, 37, jorgen mcleman, 34, joshya, 5, joshya, 88, JPagetRFPhotos, 50, Juan Gaertner, 90, Kite_rin, 35, Komsan Loonprom, 2, Konstantin Faraktinov, 75, kubais, 12, (bottom), kurhan, 39, leolintang, 64, (top), Liya Graphics, 58-59, , 68, Luis Louro, 72, mart, 108, Matt Antonio, 87, Maya2008, 53, monika3steps, Cover, (bottom left), murat5234, 64, (bottom), n_eri, 102, Nathalie Spellers Ufermann, 44, Oleksii Natykach, 81, Orla, Cover, (top left), Pagina, 54, Palau, 33, PathDoc, 23, , 83, (left), , 93, pedalist, 12, (top), Perfect Vectors, 73, Philipp Nicolai, back cover, 10, photka, 7, Pinon Road, 69, Piotr Marcinski, 61, Puwadol Jaturawutthichai, 13, Radu Bercan, 41, RedKoala, 22, Robert Adrian Hillman, 52, Robin Crossman, 105, Rocketclips, Inc, 14, Sebastian Kaulitzki, 78, Sergey Korkin, 76, SFerdon, 106, solarseven, 30-31, sss615, 85, Suzanne Tucker, 9, , 89, TinnaPong, 109, tommaso lizzul, 28, TsuneoMP, Cover, (top right), VERSUSstudio, Cover, (bottom left), Vinicius Tupinamba, 99, Vira Mylyan-Monastyrska, 66, (left), vitstudio, 21, Volt Collection, 70, whitehoune, 56-57, www.BillionPhotos.com, 38, Yayayoyo, 98, yomogi1, 11, yrchello108, 51

Design Elements by Capstone and Shutterstock

Printed in US.
092015 007526GC